The Simple Truths
of Service

Inspired by Johnny the Bagger

By Ken Blanchard & Barbara Glanz

simple truths™

TABLE OF CONTENTS

INTRODUCTION

By Ken Blanchard

Years ago you could abuse customers and they had no choice. There was nobody else doing your business. Today things are very different. If you don't take care of your customers, somebody is waiting, ready and willing to do it.

Today your competitive advantage is not the quality of your product or service. If you don't have a high quality product or service, you're not even in the game. Your competitive edge today cannot be your price, because someone can always undercut your price. What you need is a fair price. The real competitive edge you have today is how you treat your customers. The one thing your competition can't take away from you is the relationship your people have with your customers.

That's why I fell in love with Barbara Glanz's story of Johnny the Bagger. With her blessing, I've shared the story of Johnny the Bagger over and over again, everywhere I go, to illustrate that every person can make a difference for his or her customers.

Let me give you an example of the impact this story has had. Our training and consulting company was asked to develop a customer service training program for all the frontline employees involved in the opening of the new San Diego Padre Stadium, Petco Park. Since the building of the park was a controversial proposition, the top managers wanted the fans to have a very special experience in the new park. As we helped them set the customer service vision for the park, they decided that they were in the Major League memory business. Every night, every employee—whether they were in food service, maintenance, security, or what have you—was expected to focus his or her energy on creating good fan memories.

As part of the training, I made a short video, telling the story of Johnny. I ended the video looking into the camera and saying directly to every park employee, ***"Are you going to be a Johnny tonight?"*** This video was shown to everyone, no matter whether they were part-time or full-time.

A number of the department managers told me that every night before the gates opened, they would ask their people, "Are you going to be a Johnny tonight?" The first summer that Petco Park was in business, they got 7,500 unsolicited notes and letters from fans telling stories of how they had been blown away by the service they had received from someone in the park.

For example, a friend of ours ordered two fish tacos at one of the concession stands. When he got back to his seat, he took a bite and discovered that they had given him chicken tacos. Since he was yearning for fish tacos, he returned to the concession stand to exchange them. When he told the counter person what had happened, the young man's initial response was, "Let me talk to my supervisor." A more experienced worker next to him heard the conversation and said, "You don't have to ask the supervisor. This man did not get what he wanted, so give him two fish tacos. We work for him."

Another person told me his wife brought their little baby to the game one night and ran out of milk. She went to one of the concession stands and asked for some milk. A young man behind the counter said, "We don't sell milk here, but I know where I can get it. What's your seat number?" This young man got someone to cover his station while he raced out of the ballpark and down the street to a 7-11, where he bought some milk. He came back, heated the milk up, and took it to the waiting mother. She couldn't believe it.

Neither will you after you read the Johnny story and see how you and everyone in your organization can make a difference in your customers' lives. The memories you create will keep people coming back—and bringing their friends—for years to come.

JOHNNY THE BAGGER

By Barbara Glanz

As an author and a professional speaker, I travel all over the world and speak to groups about one of my favorite topics, building customer loyalty. A few years ago I was leading a customer service session for a large supermarket chain where I had the opportunity to speak to a crowd of 3,000 frontline service people—truck drivers, cashiers, baggers, produce people, stockers, floral specialists, bakers, and others.

During the course of my presentation, I said, "Every one of you can make a difference and create meaningful memories for your customers that will motivate them to come back. How?

Put your personal signature on the job.

Go home tonight and think about something you can do for your customers to make them feel special—a memory that will make them want to come back and shop at your store again."

I then directed the audience's attention to one of my personal signatures: the nearly one hundred bright-colored, handmade posters lining the walls, printed with all kinds of quotations.

Whether I'm speaking to thirty or three thousand people, I always line the walls of the room or ballroom with these posters, because they change the feeling in the room by adding color, inspiration, and fun. They take a lot of extra time to put up and they're bulky to lug around the country. But they make me stand out as a speaker and provide a wonderful memory for audiences, so it is well worth the extra effort.

A smile is a window that shows your heart is at home!

"Praise is like sunlight to the human spirit; we cannot flower and grow without it.

Jess

There are lots of ways you can give your own personal signature to your work. For example, I know a baggage attendant who decided that his personal signature would be to collect all the luggage tags that fell off customers' suitcases. In the past, the tags had been simply tossed into the garbage. The attendant decided that in his free time he would send the tags back to their owners with a note saying,

"Thank you for flying with us."

I met a graphic artist who always encloses a piece of sugarless gum in everything he sends his customers, so they never throw away anything from him. I heard of a senior manager who uses stickers and Kleenex as his personal signature. When the news is something he knows they won't like very much, he staples a piece of Kleenex to the corner of the memo.

But whenever he sends a memo with good news, he attaches a smiley face sticker.

I always leave my telephone number and e-mail address with

audiences, encouraging them to call me if they have questions or

want to share a success story they experienced by adding a personal

signature to their work. About a month after I had spoken to the

supermarket folks, I received a call from a frontline customer

contact person, *a nineteen-year-old bagger named Johnny*.

The caller, who proudly informed me that he was a Down

syndrome youngster, *told me his story*.

"Barbara, I liked what you talked about!" Johnny said excitedly, "but I didn't think I could do anything special for our customers.

After all, I'm just a bagger.

Then I had an idea." He decided that every night when he came home from work, he would find a thought for the day. "If I can't find a saying I like," Johnny said proudly, "I think one up!"

When Johnny had a good saying, his dad helped him enter his "Thought for the Day" six times on a page in the computer. Every night they printed out fifty pages. Johnny cut out each quote and signed his name on the back of every one of them. "Then I put them in a paper bag I keep beside me at work," he continued. "When I finish bagging someone's groceries, I put my thought for the day in their bag and say, 'Thanks for shopping with us.'"

It touched me to think that this young man—with a job that most people would say is not important—had made it important by creating precious memories for all his customers.

A month later the store manager called me. He said, "Barbara, you won't believe what happened today. When I was making my rounds and got up front where the cashiers are, I found the line at Johnny's checkout was three times longer than anyone else's! It went all the way down the frozen food aisle. I was concerned, so I announced, 'Get more cashiers out here; get more lanes open!' all the while trying to get people to change lanes. But no one would move. They all said, *'No, it's okay—we* want *to be in Johnny's lane— we want his 'Thought for the Day.'"*

The store manager continued, "It was a joy to watch Johnny delight the customers. I got a lump in my throat when one woman came up and grabbed my hand and said, 'I used to shop at your store only once a week, but now I come in every time I go by, because I want to get Johnny's Thought for the Day.'"

Shallots
*1.99 ea

Russet Potatoes
In-Store Special ➤ $2.99 10Lb Bag

Red Potatoes
$4.99 10Lb Bag

"I imagine that helps the bottom line," I said to the manager.

"You bet!" he replied.

Neﬁ Oranges
$5.00

RED Potatoes
PINCH and PULL

TATOES
9 5 Lb Bag
2 5 Lb Bag

"Who do you think is
the most important
person in our whole
store now?"

"Johnny, of course!"

A few months later, the store manager called me again. "Barbara," he said, "Johnny has transformed our store. Now when the floral department has a broken flower or an unused corsage, they go out on the floor and find an elderly woman or a little girl and pin it on them.

PEANUTS © United Feature Syndicate, Inc.

"One of our butchers loves Snoopy. He bought thousands of Snoopy stickers and each time he wraps a piece of meat, he puts a sticker on it. All of our cashiers now have their own personal signature. Everyone's having a lot of fun creating memories. *Our customers are talking about us...in a good way, coming back, and bringing their friends.*"

"It's not how much you do but how much love you put in to what you are doing."

— Teresa —

What a wonderful spirit of service spread throughout that store—and all because of one young man with Down syndrome who decided he could make a difference! As I tell my audiences, *"Every one of us in this room can make a difference. We can all be a Johnny."*

And with tears in nearly every eye, they agree.

The Simple Truths of Great Service

By Ken Blanchard

The following stories of great service are simple but powerful.
They're all about creating memories, building relationships, using
your unique gifts, and caring for people. No matter what your job or
position is in an organization, the real question is:

Are you going to choose to be a Johnny today?

- 1 -

Great Service Inspires Stories

A number of years ago, Sheldon Bowles and I wrote a book called *Raving Fans*.® We argued that to keep your customers today, you couldn't be content just to satisfy them; you have to create "raving fans." These are customers who are so excited about the way you treat them that they want to tell stories about you; they become part of your sales force. That's exactly what Johnny did—he created raving fan customers.

My mother, when she was 90, gave me a beautiful example of raving fan service. One day she went to her refrigerator to get some ice. When she opened the ice section, water came pouring out; something clearly was wrong. Since she was an independent cuss and wanted to solve the problem herself, she went to the Yellow Pages. She called appliance service companies one after the other, only to be told that the earliest anyone could visit her was in three weeks.

Now if you're 90 years old, three weeks is a long time. Discouraged, she was about to call me for help when she saw a little ad that said, "Same day service." She called the number and soon a friendly voice was saying, "We'd be happy to fix your refrigerator today, Mrs. Blanchard. When would you like us to come?"

"I have a choice?" my mom responded in amazement.

"Absolutely," he said.

"How about two o'clock?" Mom replied.

Not only did a serviceman show up at two, he even had tools and knew what a refrigerator was. He fixed the fridge and as he was leaving, he handed his business card to my amazed and happy mom. It had his home phone number on the back. "Anytime, night or day, you have a problem with this refrigerator, you can give me a call," he said.

What do you think my mother was doing for the next three days? She was calling everyone she knew who was still alive about the service she had received. She had become a raving fan. That's exactly how the customers in Johnny's store felt about him.

"Aim for service and success will follow."
-Albert Schweitzer-

- 2 -

Great Service Uses Outside-the-Box Thinking

One way to get customers to brag about you is to begin thinking outside the box. That's exactly what the owner of this appliance repair company my mother bragged about did. When I called him to find out how he could service people the day they called, he explained his story. It turned out that he had been a fix-it man in Massachusetts. Because of his health, his doctors suggested he move to a warmer climate. When he got to San Diego, he would find out when people were moving into a house they had just bought. He would knock on the door and tell them that he was a fix-it man. If they needed any painting or repairs done, he would be happy to do it at a reasonable price. All he asked was that they agree to refer him to other customers if they liked his work.

This guy always showed up on time, did what he said he would do with high quality, and charged a reasonable price. People loved his work. He built his business up so much that when old customers would call to get him to do something, very often he didn't have time because he was so busy. A number of people suggested to him that he start his own company. But he was reluctant, because he was concerned about managing employees and having a big payroll.

One day he woke up in the middle of the night with a brilliant idea. About thirty percent of the people living in San Diego are retirees. Many retirees are bored. They'd love to have something to do, and if they can help other people, that's even more special. So he put an ad in the local paper that said:

Retirees: If you're good at fixing things, want to help people, and make some extra money, give me a call.

It turns out he had 25-30 retirees on call every single day. So if a customer like my mother called, he had someone he could send out to her. And he didn't have the problem of a big payroll. If the people didn't work, they didn't get paid. Laughingly, he told me that he had a hard time paying some of the people, because it goofed up their Social Security. They just loved the work.

How's that for out-of-the-box thinking? Johnny didn't do too badly on that score, either.

"The best way to have a good idea is to have lots of ideas."

-Linus Pauling-

- 3 -

Great Service Is a Choice

No one can make you serve customers well. That's because great service is a choice. Years ago, my friend, Harvey Mackay, told me a wonderful story about a cab driver that proved this point. He was waiting in line for a ride at the airport. When a cab pulled up, the first thing Harvey noticed was that the taxi was polished to a bright shine. Smartly dressed in a white shirt, black tie, and freshly pressed black slacks, the cab driver jumped out and rounded the car to open the back passenger door for Harvey. He handed my friend a laminated card and said:

"I'm Wally, your driver. While I'm loading your bags in the trunk, I'd like you to read my mission statement."

Taken aback, Harvey read the card. It said:

Wally's Mission Statement:
To get my customers to their destination in the quickest, safest and cheapest way possible in a friendly environment.

This blew Harvey away. Especially when he noticed that the inside of the cab matched the outside. Spotlessly clean!

As he slid behind the wheel, Wally said, "Would you like a cup of coffee? I have a thermos of regular and one of decaf."

My friend said jokingly, "No, I'd prefer a soft drink."

Wally smiled and said, "No problem. I have a cooler up front with regular and Diet Coke, water, and orange juice."

Almost stuttering, Harvey said, "I'll take a Diet Coke."

Handing him his drink, Wally said, "If you'd like something to read, I have *The Wall Street Journal, Time, Sports Illustrated* and *USA Today*."

As they were pulling away, Wally handed my friend another laminated card. "These are the stations I get and the music they play, if you'd like to listen to the radio."

And as if that weren't enough, Wally told Harvey that he had the air conditioning on and asked if the temperature was comfortable for him. Then he advised Harvey of the best route to his destination for that time of day. He also let him know that he'd be happy to chat and tell him about some of the sights or, if Harvey preferred, to leave him with his own thoughts.

"Tell me, Wally," my amazed friend asked the driver, "have you always served customers like this?"

Wally smiled into the rearview mirror. "No, not always. In fact, it's only been in the last two years. My first five years driving, I spent most of my time complaining like all the rest of the cabbies do. Then I heard the personal growth guru, Wayne Dyer, on the radio one day. He had just written a book called *You'll See It When You Believe It.* Dyer said that if you get up in the morning expecting to have a bad day, you'll rarely disappoint yourself. He said, 'Stop complaining! Differentiate yourself from your competition. Don't be a duck. Be an eagle. Ducks quack and complain. Eagles soar above the crowd.'

"That hit me right between the eyes," said Wally. "Dyer was really talking about me. I was always quacking and complaining, so I decided to change my attitude and become an eagle. I looked around at the other cabs and their drivers. The cabs were dirty, the drivers were unfriendly, and the customers were unhappy. So I decided to make some changes. I put in a few at a time. When my customers responded well, I did more."

"I take it this has paid off for you," Harvey said.

"It sure has," Wally replied. "My first year as an eagle, I doubled my income from the previous year. This year I'll probably quadruple it.

You were lucky to get me today. I don't sit at cabstands anymore. My customers call me for appointments on my cell phone or leave a message on my answering machine. If I can't pick them up myself, I get a reliable cabbie friend to do it and I take a piece of the action."

Wally was phenomenal. He was running a limo service out of a Yellow Cab. I've probably told that story to more than fifty cab drivers over the years, and only two took the idea and ran with it. Whenever I go to their cities, I give them a call. The rest of the drivers quacked like ducks and told me all the reasons they couldn't do any of what I was suggesting.

Johnny the Bagger and Wally the Cab Driver made a different choice. They decided to stop quacking like ducks and start soaring like eagles. How about you?

"Always give the customer more than they expect."

-Nelson Boswell-

- 4 -

Great Service Starts with a Clear Vision

Great service is not an accident. It starts by deciding what kind of experience you want your customers to have—a clear vision.

In the early 1970s when everybody was going to self-service gasoline stations, my coauthor Sheldon Bowles said, "What a fabulous time to go to full service. There will be no competition." So he and his partners developed a full-service gas station called Domo Gas. They knew that if people had a choice, they certainly wouldn't choose to come to a gas station. They also knew that when customers did come, they wanted to get in and out as quickly as possible. The unique customer service vision that Sheldon and his partners imagined was an Indianapolis 500 pit stop.

All the attendants at Domo Gas were dressed up in red jumpsuits. If you drove into a Domo gas station, two or three people would race out of the hut to your car. Somebody would look under the hood, somebody would clean the windows, and somebody would start pumping gas. As Sheldon and his partners rolled out this vision in more than 150 stations across Western Canada, they killed the competition.

A gas station in northern California heard about this vision and went one step further. After serving a customer, they would hand that person a little brochure about their service that said, "P.S. We also sell gas."

Having a clear vision of great service is the key. Do you think Johnny the Bagger saw the vision Barbara painted?

"Some men see things as they are and say 'why?'
Others dream things that never were and say, 'why not?'"

-George Bernard Shaw-

- 5 -

Great Service Requires that Everyone
Catch the Vision

I'll never forget one time walking around Give Kids the World in Orlando, Florida. If a kid is dying and has never been to Disneyland, SeaWorld, MGM and the like, Give Kids the World provides that opportunity. Over the last decade, they have brought over 50,000 families to Orlando for a week at no cost to them.

The leadership of Give Kids the World decided that they were in the memory business. I was interested in how far down the organization that vision got. As I walked with the president one day, we passed a maintenance person cutting the grass. I went over to him and asked, "What business are you in here at Give Kids the World?" He smiled and said, "We make memories." I said, "How do you make memories? You just cut the grass." He said, "I don't make memories by continuing to cut the grass when a family comes by. You can always tell who the sick kid is. So I stop what I'm doing and ask the sick kid or one of his brothers and sisters if they want to help me with my chores. We make memories."

Johnny the Bagger caught the vision that Barbara had inspired. When Johnny put his quotations into a customer's bag, he was making wonderful memories for them and inspiring his associates to follow suit.

"Cherish your vision and your dreams."

-Napoleon Hill-

- 6 -

Great Service Surprises People

Over the years when I have experienced great service, I'm often caught off guard. In fact, I am surprised.

I'll never forget the story Milt Garrett told me one day. Milt, who lived at the time in Albuquerque, New Mexico, is a trainer and consultant who periodically has worked with our company. At the end of a week of training, he and his wife, Jane, took a walk on Friday night. Jane said to him, "Milt, you missed my anniversary this week."

Surprised, Milt said, "What anniversary?"

"Five years cancer free," said Jane. Five years earlier Jane had had a mastectomy. She and Milt celebrated every year that she was cancer free.

Milt felt awful. He couldn't believe he had forgotten. The week before, when he and Jane had been talking one night, they'd decided that she needed a new car. Since their son was still in college in Australia, they'd decided to wait a year until he graduated. That night, Milt said to himself, "Why am I waiting? I am so lucky that Jane is still in my life."

The next morning he called the Saturn dealership in Albuquerque and talked to one of their salespeople. I'm not kidding—the salesman's real name was Billy Graham. Milt explained the situation to Billy, saying that his kids had told him Jane really wanted a white car. "Could you get me a white Saturn by next Saturday when I get back home from training?" Milt asked.

Billy told Milt that white Saturns were hard to get. "But if you're going to come in next Saturday, I'll have one ready," he said.

The next Saturday morning Milt told Jane that he was running a bunch of errands, but he invited her to come with him so they could go out to lunch. During their drive, they passed the Saturn dealership. Milt told Jane he had to stop in for some materials because he was giving a speech about Saturn to the Chamber of Commerce. When they entered the dealership, they saw only one car: a white Saturn in the center of the showroom.

"Milt, that's the kind of car I'd love to have!" Jane said. She ran over to the Saturn and with a big grin on her face, got in. When she got out of the car and walked around the front of it, she let out a scream and began to cry. Milt had no idea what had happened. When he got to the front of the car, he saw a beautiful sign on the hood of the car that read:

Yes, Jane, this is your car! Congratulations on five years cancer free.
Love,
Milt, Billy and the whole Saturn staff.

When Billy saw them coming, he got everyone out of the showroom and into the parking lot, so that Milt and Jane could be alone. As they were crying in each other's arms, all of a sudden they heard applause. They looked up to see everyone giving them a hand. It surprised and delighted them, to say the least.

What a wonderful way to create a special moment for your customers. In many ways, that's what Johnny the Bagger did—he surprised and delighted his customers.

"We do not remember days. We remember moments in our lives."
-Unknown-

- 7 -

Great Service Begins with Anyone

When it comes to great service, everyone makes a difference. For example, what's the most common wake-up call you get in a hotel today? The phone rings but when you pick it up, there is no one there. The second most common wake-up call greets you with a recording. But again, no one is there. Today if you pick up the phone on a wake-up call and there's a human being on the other end, you hardly know what to say.

While I was staying at the Marriott in Orlando, the phone rang for my seven o'clock wake-up call. I picked it up and a woman said, "Good morning, Dr. Blanchard, this is Teresa. It's seven o'clock. It's going to be seventy-five and beautiful in Orlando today, but your ticket says you're leaving. Where are you going?"

Taken aback, I stammered, "I'm going to New York City." She countered with, "Let me look at the *USA Today* weather map. Oh, no! It's going to be forty degrees and rainy in New York today. Can't you stay?"

Now where do you think I want to stay when I go to Orlando? I want to stay at the Marriott so I can talk to Teresa in the morning! Take it from Johnny and Teresa—great service begins with anyone.

"Everyone can be great...because everyone can serve."
-Dr. Martin Luther King, Jr.-

- 8 -

Great Service Goes the Extra Mile

When people are allowed to go the extra mile for the customer, great service is the result.

Horst Schultze, one of the founders of the Ritz-Carlton Hotels, retired a few years ago as president and CEO. During Horst's reign, after orientation and extensive training, every employee was given a $2,000 discretionary fund that they could use to solve a customer problem without checking with anyone. They didn't even have to tell their boss. Horst loved to collect stories about people really using this empowerment to make a difference.

One of my favorites is about a businessman who was staying at one of the Ritz-Carlton properties in Atlanta. That day he had to fly from Atlanta to Los Angeles and then from Los Angeles to Hawaii, because the next day at one o'clock he was making a major speech to his international company. He was a little disorganized as he was leaving. On his way to the airport he discovered that he'd left behind his laptop computer, which contained all the Power Points he needed for his presentation. He tried to change his flights, but couldn't. So he called the Ritz-Carlton and said, "This is the room I was in, this is where my computer was. Have Housekeeping get it and overnight it to me. They have to guarantee delivery by ten o'clock tomorrow morning, because I need it for my one o'clock speech."

The next day Schultze was wandering around the hotel, as he often did. When he got to Housekeeping he said, "Where's Mary today?"

Her coworkers said, "She's in Hawaii."

Horst said, "Hawaii? What's she doing in Hawaii?"

He was told, "A guest left a computer in his room and he needs it for a speech today at one o'clock—and Mary doesn't trust overnight carrier services anymore." Now you might think that Mary went for a vacation, but she came back on the next plane. And what do you think was waiting for her? A letter of commendation from Horst and high fives around the hotel.

Johnny the Bagger was allowed to use the power of his imagination in serving his customers. As a result of his going the extra mile, the entire store became energized and prospered.

This reminds me of the wonderful short essay titled "And Then Some."

"AND THEN SOME...these three little words are the secret to success.

They are the difference between average people and top people in most companies.

The top people always do what is expected...and then some.

They are thoughtful of others, they are considerate and kind...and then some.

They meet their responsibilities fairly and squarely...and then some.

They are good friends and helpful neighbors...and then some.

They can be counted on in an emergency...and then some.

I am thankful for people like this, for they make the world a better place.

Their spirit of service is summed up in these three little words...

and then some."

-Carl Holmes-

- 9 -

Great Service Brings Customers Back

Truly great service will bring customers back again and again. A friend of mine understood how a store creates loyal customers when he went to Nordstrom's one day to get some perfume for his wife's birthday. The woman behind the counter said, "I'm sorry but we don't sell that perfume in our store. But I know where I can get it in the mall. How long are you going to be in our store?"

"About thirty minutes," he said.

"Fine, I'll go get it, bring it back, gift wrap it and have it ready for you when you leave." This woman literally left Nordstrom's, went to another store, got the perfume that he wanted, came back to Nordstrom's and gift wrapped it. You know what she charged him? The same price that she had paid at the other store. So Nordstrom didn't make any money on the deal but what did they make? A lifelong customer— a raving fan.

The woman who grabbed the manager's hand to tell him, "Now I come in every time I go by..." highlighted the impact Johnny was having on bringing customers back.

"A customer is the most important visitor to our premises."

-Mahatma Gandhi-

- The Final Truth -

Great Service Comes from the Heart

By Barbara Glanz

I wholeheartedly agree with Ken's Simple Truths of Great Service, but would like to add one more:

Great Service Comes from the Heart

Great customer service has to come from the inside out. You cannot mandate it. You can't threaten, reward, or coerce people to care. You can only awaken the desire and then give them the permission and encouragement to make it come alive in their work.

Simply said, if people don't have in their hearts the desire to serve and make a difference for others, they will not give great service. Mary Kay Ash, the founder of Mary Kay Cosmetics, often said that the secret of her success was hiring nice people and then allowing them to be as nice as they could be.

Johnny's idea wasn't nearly as innovative as it was loving. During my speech, I challenged him to go home and think about something he could do to make his customers feel special. He thought about that idea and framed it in a way he could understand. He didn't bother reading management books or looking for the trend of the month; he searched inside himself for a solution. What he found—his thought for the day—was real. And it came from his heart and that's the part you can't pretend.

At the core of great customer service lies the heart of each employee. When I work with an organization, I often walk around and ask people, "What is your work?" What they almost always tell me is a job description or a job title. Yet we are all so much more than that. We can bring our hearts to work with us! When you think about the question—"What is your work?"—think about this:

How is what you do every day making someone's life better?
That is your very important work!

Johnny brought his heart to his job. He focused on what he could do in his daily work to make his customers feel special and their lives a little better.

No matter what our job or position may be, we each possess a unique understanding of this world and have our own ideas and gifts to share. Our truest gift, like the one Johnny shared, can be found in our hearts if we look deeply enough and listen closely. When the heart is in the right place, the ego gets out of the way. That's when great service comes shining through.

The final truth is this:

Great service comes from the heart.

The inspiration Johnny provided didn't stop in the store. When I shared the story with my musician friend, David Roth, he was inspired to write the following song.

A Little Something More

I run a local grocery store, a friendly place to shop
One day a boy came to my market looking for a job
He said his name was Johnny, I could see that he was different
I also saw a sparkle in his eye and so I hired him.

I started him collecting carts and sweeping up the floor
In no time flat young Johnny was a bagger in my store
He took such pride and worked so hard it rubbed off on my crew
And just because he only did the best that he could do.

Johnny is a bagger in our local grocery store
Packing people's food away as they go out the automatic door
Just a job ten thousand other people do
But Johnny found a way to make it new.

Johnny came to work one Monday grinning ear to ear
He told me that his Dad was teaching him to use the home computer
Typing this and printing that, whatever he had done
The look on Johnny's face that day was brighter than the Indiana summer sun.

A couple weeks went by and I began to notice something
It started in the parking lot after people had done their shopping
They were digging through their groceries and coming out with smiles
I made a mental note and came inside to check the aisles.

The store was pretty busy, must be five o'clock, I guessed
And here the line in Johnny's lane was twice as long as all the rest
"No waiting on 1 through 4..." I said, they didn't seem to care
"We want to be in Johnny's line..." they said, and stayed right there.

That's when I discovered Johnny's magic secret brainstorm
A little note he put in every shopper's bag before they went home
And every note had what he called his "thought" for that same day
And Johnny signed the back of each good thought he gave away.

(chorus)

I can't begin to tell you how the mood in our store shifted
Whoever heard of coming home from shopping so uplifted
We see new people every day we've never seen before
And some folks say they come in now each time they pass our store.

Of course Johnny's got the longest lines of any shop in town
He's also got some syndrome that the doctors label "Down"
If you ask me how one person makes a difference any more
Come on by, see Johnny at our store.

Johnny is a bagger in our local grocery store
Packing people's food away as they go out the automatic door
And he's making things a little better than they were before
The most important person in our store
Johnny always gives a little something more!

I run a local grocery store, a friendly place to shop
One day a boy came to my market looking for a job...

KEN BLANCHARD

Few people have made a more positive and lasting impact on the day-to-day management of people and companies as Ken Blanchard. He is the author of several best-selling books, including the blockbuster international bestseller *The One Minute Manager*® and the giant business bestsellers *Leadership and the One Minute Manager, Raving Fans,* and *Gung Ho!.* His books have combined sales of more than eighteen million copies in more than twenty-five languages.

Ken is the chief spiritual officer of The Ken Blanchard Companies, a worldwide human resource development company. He is also cofounder of The Center for *FaithWalk* Leadership, a nonprofit ministry dedicated to inspiring and equipping people to walk their faith in the marketplace. Ken and his wife, Margie, live in San Diego and work with their son Scott, daughter Debbie, and Debbie's husband Humberto Medina.

For information about seminars and in-depth consulting in the areas of leadership, teamwork, customer service, performance management and organizational synergy, please visit www.kenblanchard.com or call 1-800-728-6000. For information on The Center for *FaithWalk* Leadership, visit www.leadlikejesus.com.

BARBARA GLANZ

Barbara Glanz, CSP, works with organizations to improve morale, retention and service, and with people who want to rediscover the joy in their work and in their lives. She has presented on six continents and in all 50 states since 1995. Known as the business speaker who speaks to your heart as well as to your head, Barbara is the author of *Balancing Acts—More Than 250 Guiltfree, Creative Ideas to Blend Your Work and Your Life, Handle with CARE—Motivating and Retaining Employees, CARE Packages for the Workplace—Dozens of Little Things You Can Do to Regenerate Spirit at Work, The Creative Communicator, CARE Packages for the Home,* and *Building Customer Loyalty.*

For six years she was the manager of training and director of quality in training for Kaset International, a Times Mirror firm that has been helping organizations become more customer-focused for over 25 years. As an internationally known speaker, trainer and business consultant, who has a Master's degree in Adult Education, Barbara lives and breathes her personal motto: "Spreading Contagious Enthusiasm.™"

For more information, visit www.barbaraglanz.com. Barbara can be reached at 941-312-9169; Fax 941-349-8209; or by email at bglanz@barbaraglanz.com